IMAGES OF SCOTLAND

GRANGEMOUTH

An aerial view of Grangemouth. The entire dock complex can be seen from high above the River Forth looking to the south. In the foreground, on the left, is the present entrance lock, overlooked by the control centre and pilots' headquarters on the quayside. This large lock can accommodate vessels of up to 30,000 tons and is operable at almost all states of the tide. To the right of the new entrance lock is its predecessor. Beyond is the twisting, muddy course of the River Carron, navigated by vessels during the nineteenth century to enter the Carron Dock pictured in the background. In the foreground the oil tank farms can be seen, these are connected with the BP-Amoco Oil Refinery, partially visible on the left bank of the Grange Burn. In the far background the M9 motorway separates Grangemouth from the green belt that lies between it and Falkirk; some of this town's multi-storey tower blocks can be seen rising skyward on the edge of the Braes. (Forth Ports plc)

IMAGES OF SCOTLAND

GRANGEMOUTH

WILLIAM F. HENDRIE

The
History
Press

To my late father, Nelson Patrick Hendrie, who was very proud to be a Portonian and whose many stories and recollections inspired this book. Also to my cousin Maude whose patience and constant encouragement were an enormous help to me while compiling this book.

Acknowledgements

I would like to thank the many Portonians who have helped with photographs and information for this book. In particular I wish to thank Maude Binnie, Elizabeth Crampsey, Helen Elder, Ian Elder, Margaret Glen, Isabel McNab, John Mitchel, Gilbert Peddie and Bill Strathearn and all the volunteers at the Grangemouth Heritage Centre whose comprehensive collection of photographs feature in the following pages. My thanks also to Guthrie Pollock and my editor at Tempus Publishing, Campbell McCutcheon, whose mother, Barbara, is a Portonian, for their help with the layout of this book.

First published in 2002 by Tempus Publishing Limited

Reprinted in 2008 by
The History Press
The Mill, Brimscombe Port
Stroud, Gloucestershire, GL5 2QG
www.thehistorypress.co.uk

British Library Cataloguing in Publication Data.
A catalogue record for this book is available from the British Library.

ISBN 978 0 7524 2124 7

Typesetting and origination by Tempus Publishing Limited
Printed in Great Britain

Contents

An aerial view looking north across the River Forth to the shores of Fife where the tall tower of the coal-fired Longannet Power Station provides a readily identifiable landmark. Directly opposite the pier at Longannet lie the old dock gates and to their right the new entrance to the port. Grangemouth is the busiest port on the east coast of Scotland and many of its facilities can be identified. These include the tanks of the oil farms associated with Grangemouth's largest employers, the BP-Amoco Oil Refinery and petro-chemicals complex, also the powerful hoists of the container berths and, on the far side of the dock basin, the modern Baltic timber products warehouse. On either side of the docks lie the River Carron to the left and the Grange Burn to the right, both flowing northwards until their waters merge with that of the Forth. (Forth Ports plc)

Introduction

Grangemouth is one of a small number of towns in Scotland whose exact date of origin can be stated. On 10 July 1768, local laird Laurence Dundas dug his spade deep into the grassy shore of the River Carron, half a mile inland from where it joins the River Forth. He ceremonially cut the first turf to mark where the eastern end of the proposed Forth & Clyde Canal was to commence its thirty-nine mile route across the narrow waist of Central Scotland to Bowling on the River Clyde.

For the powerful Dundas it was a moment of triumph; originally the eastern end of the canal was planned to be at the already established port of Borrowstounness, the 'Burgh Town on the Nose of Land', or Bo'ness as it became known, five miles further down the Forth. Indeed, a stretch of the new canal had already been excavated west from Kinneil and a few remains of its course can still be identified. However, the enterprising Dundas realised the commercial importance of the canal and, thanks to his 'wheeling and dealing', the eastern terminus was moved to his Stirlingshire estate where it was originally known simply as Sea Lock. In 1771 a plan was published using the title *The Sea Lock at Grange Burn Mouth* and, when Sir Thomas Dundas succeeded his father in 1781, he indicated that he preferred this title as it incorporated the name of the little river that flowed through his lands. Grange Burn Mouth was soon shortened and within two years the name Grangemouth was common usage.

In 1790 the Forth & Clyde Canal was completed and Grangemouth's harbour soon became very popular. Ships were able to unload their cargoes straight into canal barges ready for onward transportation and the popularity this engendered facilitated the site's successful application for its own Custom House. This was a very significant development as it made the new port entirely independent of neighbouring Bo'ness.

Grangemouth's trading dominance continued in the 1840s and '50s with the advent of the railway. Rail superseded the canal as the preferred means of inland transport and the flat landscape of the new port, much of which was reclaimed from the waters of the River Forth, made it much easier to build new tracks. Bo'ness, by comparison, was tightly hemmed in by the old, steep, raised beaches of the Forth and rail access was limited to a single line.

The undeveloped and spacious flat land that Grangemouth occupied was also far more appealing to the new industries of Victorian Britain than the already crowded coastal strip at Bo'ness. This appeal continued throughout Victorian times and grew further until the British Transport Commission closed the docks at Bo'ness in 1959, leaving Grangemouth to prosper as Scotland's second most important seaport.

During the 1950s Grangemouth enjoyed its fastest decade of growth, as it became Scotland's oil boom town with the enormous growth of the British Petroleum Oil Refinery and its associated industries. Together, these industries are Scotland's largest source of employment and the largest payers of local taxes in the country.

Grangemouth's link with oil goes back to the nineteenth century when cargoes of whale blubber were discharged at the port and subsequently boiled to produce oil. Its connection with the modern oil business came in the 1930s when Scottish Oils, which traditionally produced their products by refining shale rock in neighbouring West and Mid Lothian, decided to hedge its bets by also importing oil from the Persian Gulf in the Middle East. Grangemouth was selected as the most convenient port to discharge these first cargoes of foreign oil on the basis that, if the venture proved uneconomic, the new refinery could easily revert to processing crude from the Scottish shale industry. In 1939, the outbreak of the Second World War, and the resultant interference with shipping, halted the growth of the new refinery. It was not until the late 1940s that the expansion plans got underway that ultimately earned Grangemouth the nickname of 'Scotland's Boom Town'.

Today Grangemouth still continues to expand but at a slower rate. It offers its inhabitants many excellent facilities; from the modern La Porte Precinct shopping centre to modern schools and sports facilities that are among the best in Scotland. This book gives both Portonians, as those born and bred in the town are known, and newcomers alike an insight into how the place they have chosen to make their home has developed over almost 250 years. It begins by looking at Grangemouth's throbbing heart; its long-established and highly successful port.

One

The Port

The history of Grangemouth Docks as Scotland's second most important seaport dates back to 1843 when it was decided by the Forth & Clyde Canal Co. that it was no longer acceptable to have vessels left high and dry in the harbour at low tide.

As a result its first proper dock was officially opened on Wednesday 12 July. The first ship to sail through the lock gates, which guaranteed sufficient depth of water in the dock at all states of the tide, was the SS *Hampton*. The steamer had been forced to lie off in the river since her arrival the previous Friday because of problems with the new dock gates but six days later, her entry into the dock went without a hitch. As she berthed with the help of the steam paddle tug *Harmony*, the firing of several small cannon and the enthusiastic cheers of a 5,000 strong crowd greeted her.

Included in the crowd were the navvies, the labourers who had spent five years excavating the dock basin. They were rewarded with pies washed down with pints of porter, but the management of the New Dock, as it was originally known, instructed that the cost must not exceed one shilling for each man. At the same time the dignitaries at the opening retired to the Zetland Arms Inn, where they wined and dined late into the night with many toasts to Queen Victoria and Prince Albert, to the Earl and Countess of Zetland and to Mr Lock, the local MP. The captain of the *Hampton* was not invited but was entertained instead by the harbour master, Mr Henry Rodger, at the Crown Inn.

On 20 July the *Hampton* sailed again for America. Many other vessels followed her into the New Dock at Grangemouth and trade at the port was so brisk that by 1855, it was decided that a second dock was required. Named the Junction Dock, it was opened in October 1859.

By the 1880s, even with the two docks in constant use, the port could barely cope with all the ships waiting to discharge and load and with the many vessels lying off in the roads waiting for a berth. For several years Caledonian Railway had been eager to acquire a port on the east coast of Scotland but it took until 1877 to complete a deal with the original owners, the canal company.

The outcome was the excavation of the Carron Dock. Covering an area of 19 $\frac{4}{}$ acres, all dug from land reclaimed from the river, the entrance lock was 350ft long with a depth of 26ft. The new dock opened on 3 June 1882 and was equipped with the most modern cranes and hydraulic coal hoists. As well as providing bunkering facilities for ships requiring fuel for their furnaces, coal was Grangemouth's largest export at the time and each hoist could cope with eighty-five railway wagon loads, each weighing 80 tons, every day.

Trade continued to expand and in October 1898 work began on the very large Grange Dock, also dug from land reclaimed from the Forth. The most modern dredgers from the Netherlands, known locally as the Dutch Blowers, because they could blow away as well as suck up the mud, were brought to the port. However, progress was slower than expected and because of difficulties in finding firm foundations for the new dock gates, the opening was delayed until October 1906. Salvesen Line's RMS *Norway* was the first vessel to enter the new dock, her bows breaking a blue ribbon as they passed through the inner gate.

Forty miles of railway sidings serviced the new dock and the hydraulic coal hoists could handle 12-ton wagons. The following year modernisation took another step forward when hydraulic capstans were installed thereby dispensing with the forty horses and their drivers who had formerly been a familiar part of the scene in the port.

In 1914 the port was requisitioned by the Admiralty on the outbreak of war and named HMS *Rameses* under the command of Admiral L. Clinton-Baker. Many naval personnel were stationed in the town and the YMCA building in Abbots Road was taken over as a dormitory for the Wrens. Among the naval vessels based in the docks were the famous Q-Ships under Cdr Campbell. These were merchant ships converted to carry concealed guns and who acted as decoys to lure enemy U-boats into attacking them.

The port re-opened to commercial shipping in December 1918 and trade continued during the 1920s and '30s until the outbreak of war in 1939 inevitably caused a setback. Later, with peace returned and the election of a Labour government, the port was nationalised under the control of the British Transport Commission and oil replaced timber as the main import.

Further change occurred when Grangemouth became the first port in Britain to be able to handle containers after the erection of two huge 25-ton hoists in May 1966. Around this time it was also provided with a 'ro-ro' berth which enabled tractors produced by the British Leyland plant at Blackburn, near Bathgate, to roll onto ferries for export while similar vessels brought imports of foreign cars.

Now owned by the enterprising Forth Ports Plc, Grangemouth continues to be known as one of the country's most efficient ports. It has a dedicated workforce capable of producing the fastest possible turnarounds for all types of vessels from oil tankers to liquid petroleum gas tankers, from box ships to bulk carriers.

Lighthouse and S.S. Orient, Grangemouth.

This squat, whitewashed lighthouse formerly guided ships up the River Carron on their approach to the original entrance to the docks at Grangemouth. Beyond can be seen the Ochil Hills. The steamer on the right about to enter port is the SS *Orient*. Portonians of the older generation still speak fondly of summer outings to the dock gates where they used to enjoy picnics on the appropriately named Shelly Bank.

Cargo vessels from the Victorian period berthed in the original harbour at Grangemouth and left high and dry at low tide.

Carron Line, whose ships were all registered in the port of Grangemouth, took its name from the river on whose banks the company's famous iron works were deliberately sited in 1759. This was in order to make use of waterways, at the time the most efficient form of transport. As well as supplying the iron works with raw materials and shipping its finished products to market, the Carron Line vessels also provided a regular passenger service to London from both Grangemouth and Bo'ness.

CARRON LINE S.S. GRANGE. GRANGEMOUTH

Picture postcard sold by the purser aboard Carron Line's SS *Grange* to passengers keen to have a souvenir of their voyage to post to their relatives and friends. While travellers nowadays consult air and rail timetables when considering a trip to London, a century ago it was the tide tables which dictated the arrival and departure of the Carron ships on their journeys to and from the capital. Two classes of travel were available: first class, in which passengers enjoyed the privacy and comfort of their own cabins, and the more economical steerage, so named because this communal accommodation was situated in the stern of the vessel over the rudders and propeller. The 263-ton *Grange* is depicted sailing out of the old dock gates at Grangemouth at the beginning of one of her twice-weekly round trips to the Thames.

Carron Line named many of its vessels after rivers. Other ships included the 498-ton *Forth*, the 454-ton *Thames*, the 400-ton *Clyde*, the 447-ton *Carron*, the 389-ton *Derwent* and the 554-ton *Avon*.

Another shipping company with very close links with Grangemouth was the Gibson Rankine Line, whose well-known skipper, Capt. Mercer Scobbie, is pictured here. When he was not at sea, Capt. Scobbie lived with his wife Nancy at home in Grangemouth. They resided for many years at Garfield House that still stands in Abbotsgrange Road.

The *Grangemouth*, one of the vessels of the Gibson Rankine Line that Capt. Scobbie skippered, seen here with her tall, black funnel.

The port of Grangemouth as it looked shortly after the completion of the Carron Dock in 1882. The dock was named after the River Carron that vessels had to sail up to enter through the lock. Although not used for a century, the lock survives and is still used as one of the port's dry docks. The Carron Dock occupies a twenty-acre site and can accommodate vessels with a draught up to 25ft.

The largest of Grangemouth's docks, the thirty-acre Grange Dock shortly before its completion in 1906. On the left is the swing bridge constructed to span the channel that connects it with the older Carron Dock.

During the early years of the twentieth century Grangemouth was a popular bunkering port for steamers. They knew that they could always rely on plentiful supplies of good coal, mainly from the Lanarkshire coalfield. It was brought by rail to Grangemouth because the dock was equipped with the very latest 36-ton coal hoists. During fuelling operations each ship was served by two of these powerful hoists that were capable of emptying the entire contents of a coal wagon in one speedy operation.

A steamer discharges cargo in the Grange Dock shortly after its completion in 1906. Notice the hoists on the quayside on the left and the two other vessels getting up steam prior to sailing from the port

Grangemouth was involved in the whale-oil industry between 1850 and 1870, but this was not one of the whales caught during a voyage to the Arctic. It was in fact landed on the quayside during the 1920s after it mistakenly swam up the River Forth and became trapped in the docks. Despite efforts to save it, the whale died and the disposal of it posed a considerable problem for the local authorities. Another whale swam through the entrance lock and entered the docks during the 1950s but eventually became trapped and died in the entrance to the Forth & Clyde Canal. A century earlier the blubber of the whales caught by the Grangemouth Arctic fishers was boiled to obtain its oil at a small refinery situated near Nelson Street. Today the raw material for the BP-Amoco refinery at Grangemouth comes once more from the North Sea, not in the form of blubber from whales, but as crude oil delivered by the pipeline which comes ashore at Kinneil Bay.

Another of Grangemouth's industries was shipbuilding and the Grangemouth Dockyard Co. became one of the best known yards on the Forth. The most famous vessel constructed at Grangemouth was also one of the earliest, the pioneering *Charlotte Dundas*, the world's first practical steamship. Launched in 1801, eleven years before the Clyde-built *Comet*, she was designed by Dumfriesshire inventor William Symington. He enjoyed the patronage of Lord Dundas of Kerse who persuaded him that his innovative vessel should be constructed at Grangemouth so that her trials could take place on the Forth & Clyde Canal.

The *Charlotte Dundas* was 56ft long with a beam of 18ft and a draught of 8ft and cost £7,000 to construct. She was equipped with a steam engine that had a cylinder of 22in diameter and a piston-driven stern wheel. During experimental voyages throughout 1802 and 1803 the *Charlotte Dundas* proved powerful enough to tow two fully laden 70-ton barges, the *Active* and the *Euphemia*. However, the canal authorities became very concerned that the wash from the steamer's stern paddle wheel was damaging the banks and so ordered a halt to the trials. The *Charlotte Dundas* was consequently laid up at Bainsford between Grangemouth and Falkirk and never sailed again.

The *Charlotte Dundas* is still remembered in Grangemouth through its inclusion as a symbol on the town's coat of arms and the bequeathing of its name to this shopping centre. (Arthur Down)

The familiar profile of the offices of the Grangemouth Dockyard Co. reflected in the still waters of the Forth & Clyde Canal, long before it was filled in to make way for a road. The dockyard seen at the height of its prosperity with the crane towering over the bows of a large cargo vessel taking shape on the stocks. Once completed the Grangemouth yard launched its vessels into the River Carron. The narrowness of the Carron added to the difficulties of the operation as ships had to be launched sideways into the water.

The dockyard was decked with flags to mark the occasion of the launch of the cargo ship SS *Ganet* that had just been completed on the stocks. Of particular interest is the large banner in the foreground that, as well as the Union flag and the Lion Rampant, displays the yard's name and the symbols for Grangemouth. These include the antlered deer and the *Charlotte Dundas*, whose construction was the yard's first claim to fame.

The cargo ship *Palomares* nearing completion on the stocks at the Grangemouth Dockyard Co. The Grangemouth yard built many cargo vessels for foreign owners including several in Malta, Portugal and Iceland.

The *Palomares* is launched into the River Carron.

Riveters, platers and other workers at the Grangemouth Dockyard Co., all wearing their flat bunnets, waiting patiently on Friday afternoon to receive their weeks wages in cash at the end of their shift. Money for the wage packets was collected by the office staff each Friday morning and paid out later in the day through the windows of the company's offices in Canal Street, different trades being paid at different windows.

Carron Dry Dock was created out of the original entrance from the River Carron.

Ship repairs also kept the Grangemouth yard steadily occupied. In this Edwardian photograph the foreign sailing vessel *Ida IV*, registered in Groningen in the Netherlands, is seen in the yard's dry dock. The recession in the British shipbuilding industry in the 1960s and '70s brought an end to ship-building for every yard on the Scottish east coast, but ship repairing still takes place at Grangemouth.

Described as a rotor ship (i.e. turbine-powered), the *Buckau* attracted the attention of the photographer as this was her first call at Grangemouth.

The largest steel sheet ever exported from Grangemouth being raised by crane from the quayside during the 1930s while the port's dockers look on. Manufactured at Colville's famous steelworks at Motherwell, it was transported by rail to Grangemouth where it was handled by well-known local stevedore firm David Trail & Sons who were in competition with Palmers & Simpson & Sharp. According to the statistics painted onto the steel this huge sheet weighed 15 tons and measured a massive 47ft 8in by 13ft 7in and was 1ft thick. (Isabel McNab)

A view over the rail bridge at Station Brae in the 1930s looking north towards the River Carron over the dock whose cranes jut skywards.

During the years following the Second World War railway wagons were slowly replaced by road transport. (Forth Ports plc)

This Hapag Lloyd Line ship was one of the first to bring containers to Grangemouth, but there is also still much general cargo on the quayside waiting to be loaded. (Forth Ports plc)

Seen here sailing through the new entrance lock to the port, the *Doulos* was an unusual visitor to Grangemouth during the 1980s. This former passenger ship was one of two vessels specially converted by an evangelical Christian organisation into a floating Bible bookshop. Her smaller sister ship the *Logos* also visited the port and during their stays they were open to the public. While aboard visitors not only had the opportunity to buy a wide range of religious books but also their volunteer crews organised tours of the two vessels. This helped raise funds for their more usual tours of under-developed countries in Africa, Asia and the West Indies. Other passenger vessels to visit Grangemouth during the 1960s were the two 12,000-ton school ships, *Dunera* and *Devonia*. These took thousands of local school pupils on cruises across the North Sea to the Scandinavian countries. Pupils from Grangemouth Academy sailed on these exciting voyages and many adult members of the community also took the opportunity to sail on National Trust for Scotland cruises which were arranged on the two vessels during school summer holiday periods. (Forth Ports plc)

In the picture on the previous page, tugs can be seen guiding the *Doulos* through the entrance lock. In 2000 the tugs of the Forth Towing Co. were taken over by Dutch owners WIJS Muller. Here they are seen in their smart new livery of white superstructure and bright blue and black hulls with blue funnels capped by white and black rings, but still bearing their original names of the *Forth* and the *Dundas*. Both tugs have a tonnage of 187 tons. (Arthur Down)

The docks look comparatively quiet in September 2000 with only two vessels being worked. In reality this appearance is created by improved work practices leading to ever-faster turnaround times and the port is busier than it has ever been with record-breaking tonnage. (Arthur Down)

A few moments after the previous picture was taken a heavily laden box ship sails into the container berth on her weekly visit to the Grangemouth, confirmation of the busy nature of the dock. (Arthur Down)

Grangemouth's traditional import of timber products still continues and Finn Timber, with its distinctive wooden tree symbol, is one of the leading firms in this line of business. (Arthur Down)

A fishmeal processing plant is another modern addition to the firms based in the port of Grangemouth. It processes catches of tiny sand eels, caught further down river in the Firth of Forth and turns them into protein-rich animal feed. (Arthur Down)

Grangemouth's original dock was known as the Junction Dock as it provided access to the Forth & Clyde Canal whose entrance lock can be seen in the background.

Sailing ships and steamers in the Junction Dock during the early 1900s. The buildings of Grangemouth's Old Town can be seen in the background. The building of the Queens Hotel and the old Town Hall with its clock tower still stands but most of the other premises have been demolished.

Canal Street. Behind the two storey, stone-built, slate-roofed houses rise the tall cranes of the Grangemouth Dockyard Co. that built many fine ships in Grangemouth. Models of some of them and pictures of most may be seen in the Grangemouth Heritage Centre at Zeneca House, formerly the Imperial Function Suite. One of the wooden bascule bridges over the canal that could be raised to allow the passage of the barges can be seen in the centre.

Grangemouth derived its original name of Sealock from the first lock at the entrance to the Forth & Clyde Canal. The work of digging the canal across Central Scotland began in July 1768 and took squads of labourers twenty-two years to excavate its entire thirty-five mile length to Bowling on the River Clyde. The canal was designed by engineer John Smeaton and its construction included a five-mile Monkland extension, dug to provide increased access to the Glasgow hinterland, a rich source of heavy cargoes. The labourers who worked on the canal were known as navvies as it was said that they navigated its course from the Forth to the Clyde. Many were immigrants from the south of Ireland and others came from the Highlands of Scotland, lured south by the promise of regular work and pay. Here barges awaited cargo at the entrance to the canal. Across the calm waters of the basin can be seen two of Grangemouth's many public houses that thrived on the uncouth trade provided by the many sailors who visited the port. This area was also frequented by the famous Dock Fairies, the accommodating 'ladies of the night'. They are said to have done a brisk trade despite threats of arrest from the local constabulary whose police offices and cells were at this time situated in the Old Town near the Queens Hotel.

A boy plays on a raft of timber logs, just beyond Canal Street, the houses of which are reflected in the still waters of the canal. In the distance three barges can be seen moored along the towing path in front of the houses. The narrow pedestrian crossing over the top of the lock gates was known locally as 'the Splash'. On the way home from the local pubs on Friday and Saturday nights, it was not uncommon for users of this short cut to lose their balance and fall into the water.

One of the many wooden bascule bridges over the Forth & Clyde Canal seen in detail during the 1920s. This bridge spanned the canal at Dalgrain Road and carried traffic travelling between Grangemouth and the outlying village of Glensburgh. The motor bus in the picture provided a regular public service on this route.

An RNLI lifeboat was an unusual visitor to Grangemouth having sailed through the Forth & Clyde Canal. Although Grangemouth has never had its own lifeboat, the nearest being stationed fifteen miles down-river near the Forth Bridge at the Hawes Pier at Queensferry, as a port town its inhabitants have always given strong financial support to the good work of the Royal National Lifeboat Institute.

A picture postcard view of the hamlet of Glensburgh.

This bascule bridge has been raised to allow a 'puffer' to pass through after unloading its cargo at Grangemouth Docks. During the first sixty years of the canal's existence it carried many small passenger ships. Until the opening of the railways in the 1840s and 1850s these vessels provided the fastest means of travel to and from Glasgow. Many 'puffers' such as this one were built on the canal at Kirkintolloch. Although this vessel is steam powered, many of the vessels which plied its smooth waters, especially in earlier years, were horse-drawn barges and the towing path can be seen clearly on the left of the picture. It is edged with what were known as kicking stones to keep the horses clear of the edge. The circular white-washed house was the toll-house where dues were collected from vehicles using the bridge.

Between Glensburgh and the neighbouring village of Skinflats the Old Pay Brig carried the road over the River Carron. As the name suggests travellers originally had to pay a toll.

These girls feeding the swans are standing on a stretch of the towing path on the banks of the Forth & Clyde Canal between Glensburgh and Earl's Gates, so called because they marked the entrance to the Earl of Zetland's mansion, Kerse House. This was the home of Grangemouth's founders, the Dundas family, who were responsible for the building of the Old Town.

Two

The Old Town

Grangemouth Old Town was planned by Sir Laurence Dundas. His grand idea was to create a model town built, appropriately for its setting, in the shape of a ship, with fine broad streets stretching all the way from 'bow' to 'stern'. Unfortunately, Sir Laurence died in 1781 before much of his scheme was turned into reality. However, his successor maintained the high standards and the town which arose over the next two decades was provided with streets 40ft wide and with house fronts strictly in line much like Edinburgh's Georgian New Town. As in the capital the buildings in Grangemouth's Old Town were well constructed with walls of sandstone and roofs of Scottish grey slate with stoutly built chimney breasts for their coal fires. While these buildings were not on the rich, almost aristocratic scale of Edinburgh's George Street and Charlotte Square, they were all well finished dwellings whose walls were decorated with stone carved ropes, scrolls and other mouldings of a more elaborate nature than might have been expected of artisan housing.

   As well as houses, the Old Town's two main thoroughfares, Grange Street and South Bridge Street, also boasted spacious shops and pubs while the latter was dominated by the spire of the town clock. Below it were the original burgh chambers, from whose offices the town was administered, and adjoining it were the police station, burgh court and the jail. Its cells were a deterrent to rowdy behaviour by local lads and foreign sailors alike.

Looking east along the length of South Bridge Street towards where the spire of the Old Town Clock still stands. In front is the balustraded facade of the Queen's Hotel where the captains of the ships gathered to meet their port agents and where business deals were done while enjoying a drink at the bar. It must often have been late before they left to make their way back aboard their vessels, but fortunately the streets of Grangemouth's Old Town were well lit by gas lamps, seen on the left. Grangemouth Gas Works was one of the first in Scotland when it was opened in 1836, ten years before Falkirk. The first gas streetlights were set up near the Dockyard in 1867, but gas had been used for lighting in the port before this time. In 1905 gas street lighting was improved greatly by the introduction of a new type of incandescent burner.

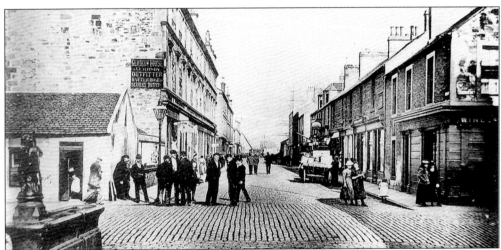

Grange Street connected with South Bridge Street and ran at right angles to it. Looking north along its cobbled surface towards the port, the masts of sailing ships can be glimpsed in the background. Many businesses in the old town depended on the trade these vessels brought, from the public house on the corner to the Glasgow House Outfitters opposite it on the left. Round the corner from it are Galloway the baker's original premises with one of the bakers standing in the doorway. My grandfather William Fyfe Hendrie founded the family's drapery and millinery business in premises in Grange Street before opening a branch in the Baltic Chambers in Lumley Street, now La Porte Precinct in the New Town.

Another of the Old Town's thoroughfares, North Basin Street, is seen on the far side of the Forth & Clyde Canal in this picture postcard view.

South Bridge Street again, looking west, over the original wooden bascule bridge that spanned the Forth & Clyde Canal. Beyond the bridge, to the left, are the Town Clock and the front of the Queen's Hotel. On the opposite side of the street is a large pile of Baltic timber. Much of the timber unloaded at Grangemouth was processed by the town's own sawmills thus bringing much prosperity to the town. However, ships in the Junction Dock on the right could also unload their cargoes directly into barges for onward shipment to users in the west of Scotland. In Grangemouth the logs were stored in the town's famous timber basins that have now been filled in, but for older residents they will always be remembered as unofficial swimming pools in summer and ice rinks in winter. The premises on the corner housed the offices of William Glen, the printer who provided the town with its first local newspaper, *The Grangemouth Advertiser*, which a century later is still published every week. The Falkirk-based Johnston Press, Britain's leading publisher of local papers, now owns it.

Kerse House was the home of the Dundas family who painstakingly planned the building of the Old Town. It stood to the west of where the roundabout at Earl's Gates is situated and the ICI Recreation Club, whose name has been changed recently to the Earl's Gates Recreation Club, stands on the site of the house's large walled garden. Parts of the mansion dated back to 1625 and its owners were loyal supporters of the reigning House of Stewart. Later, after the Glorious Revolution of 1689 and the accession to the throne of William and Mary of Orange, the sympathy of the Dundas family remained with the exiled Stewarts and the Jacobite cause. However, during the period after the Act of Union in 1707, Sir Laurence Dundas was one of the Scottish entrepreneurs who benefitted greatly from the opportunities for trade and commerce that came with it. In 1745 he supported the Hanoverian Government side in the Jacobite Rebellion and added greatly to his status by organising all of the troops for the Duke of Cumberland's army at the Battle of Culloden. The following year he was elected Member of Parliament at Westminster for the neighbouring constituency of Linlithgowshire, but in 1748 returned to military service to support King George's brother, Cumberland, fighting in Flanders. From 1756 to 1763, during what later became known as the Seven Years War, he acquired both fame and fortune by ensuring the British troops were kept well supplied. His reward was a baronetcy, awarded in 1762. His beautiful home, with its balustraded terraces sloping down to extensive lawns and gardens, was demolished many years ago.

Kerse Avenue, one of the approach roads to the Dundas' stately home, Kerse House, whose entrance at Earl's Gates can be seen in the background. The two young girls stand outside one of the cottages built to house the estate's many workers. Stone built, it had a roof of red pantiles imported from the Netherlands and this particular view was sold in newsagents and stationers shops in Grangemouth as a Christmas card.

Grangemouth's firemen pose beside their early horse-drawn fire appliance at the Earl's Gates. Later, in 1902, Grangemouth became the first town in Stirlingshire to acquire a steam fire engine.

The popular Grange Manor Hotel that now attracts many visitors to Earl's Gates. Owned by Bill and Jane Wallace, the hotel has been developed around the attractive stone built house that was originally the home of the factor of the Kerse Estate. As well as the main dining room in the house, the Grange Manor also offers guests the choice of informal dining in the former stables which still stands in the hotel's spacious grounds. (Arthur Down).

This bascule bridge used to connect the Old Town to the New Town. Beyond the bridge on the left in Station Road is Hay's stable from which horses and carriages could be hired. Also on the left is a large pile of the timber on whose import much of Grangemouth's early prosperity was based.

Three

The New Town

While the Old Town was designed to conform to the requirements for a model town, the expansion deemed essential had plans that were even more ambitious. The intention with the New Town was to make it one of the new wave of Garden Cities. It was with this lofty aim in mind that, when work began on the New Town in 1861, the Dundas family, as superiors of the fues, insisted that every house must have a garden.

During the following decades the New Town began to expand east from the Forth & Clyde Canal to the Grange Burn. Up until the end of the First World War the Dundas Estate strictly controlled all planning applications. Authority then passed to Grangemouth Town Council which was equally diligent in ensuring standards and many Portonians regretted when it had to surrender this power to Stirling County Council whose members had less local interest. By this time however Grangemouth was already well established as one of the most forward-looking towns in Britain with a second fine, new Town Hall, a first-class public library, a spacious drill hall and the fine Zetland Park with its excellent leisure and sports facilities.

By 1900 Grangemouth had a population of 5,000 and the New Town expanded further east to where Inch House had originally been. Surrounded by fields, it became the home of Bailie MacPherson and later of the Hendrie family from whom the author is descended. More fine detached and semi-detached, well-built stone villas began to be erected beyond the Burn Bridge along the length of Bo'ness Road as far out as Avondhu, built in impressive Scottish baronial style. Later came streets of mainly single storey bungalows, such as those in Ronaldshay Crescent, that took its name from the interest of the Dundas family in the Northern Isles. They were built in the latest styles and were subsequently added to by the further development of flats in streets such as Victoria Road, whose varieties of well-built homes still make interesting walks around the New Town, and of whose prosperity and expansion they are a lasting illustration.

The New Town of Grangemouth seen from the air looking from the south-west. Looking over the railway lines, the closest street is Union Road. Parallel to it is Dundas Street. Beyond that are the tenement homes of Lumley Street and Kerse Road, which run at right angles to the former. The tree lined banks of the Grange Burn and the new homes on Bo'ness Road can also be seen. On the opposite bank of the curving course of the Grange Burn lie the waters of the docks and a corner of the River Carron can be glimpsed in the top left hand corner.

The housing seen in this picture postcard view of Talbot Street is middle class with two-storey detached and semi-detached houses. On the right past the bowling green the two-storey block of houses has been demolished and Talbot House old folks' centre now stands on the site. Most of the attractive stone built homes on the left still stand.

This picture postcard gives an excellent idea of how Lumley Street originally looked with its long lines of two-storey, stone-built, slate-roofed terraced tenements. The fact that there is an absence of smoke rising from the rows of chimney pots suggests a warm summer day when there were no coal fires burning in the grates of the fireplaces in the rooms below. If the weather was warm the visit from the lemonade lorry parked on the left hand side of the street would no doubt be particularly welcome as it delivered soft drinks manufactured by Boyd's in the neighbouring town of Bo'ness. In the foreground on the left the hooped red and white pole jutting out over the pavement advertises the barber's shop, where the men who lived in the surrounding houses could have their hair cut.

Similar crowded, working class homes also lined both sides of neighbouring Marshall Street. Again the impressive width and straightness of the road is worth noting.

Talbot Street showing the facade of the Territorial Army Hall, known locally as the Drill Hall as it was here the local army volunteers met weekly to hold regular drill sessions. The volunteers formed in 1860 and initially met in the old Town Hall in the Old Town until their own headquarters seen in this picture was completed in 1887, the year of Queen Victoria's Golden Jubilee. The hall has been demolished and garages and a car park now occupy the site.

Recalling when each winter the Grange Burn frequently burst its banks. The pancake-flat nature of the site on which the New Town was built allowed the floods to spread rapidly and here householders can be seen wading through the water in Talbot Street. The problem continued until the Grange Burn Pumping scheme was completed. Looking along Talbot Street, in the background to the east can be seen the spire of the Grange Church on the corner of Park Road and Ronaldshay Crescent. The foundation stone of the church was laid on 6 August 1910. The building still dominates the scene but it is no longer used for worship and has been converted into attractive apartments. On the right hand side of the picture can be glimpsed Mr R.G.D. Hood's photographic studio.

Mr. Hood's small, two-storey photographic studio originally stood in Lumley Street beside other well known Grangemouth businesses. They include Mr W.N. Dollar's chemists shop, whose traditional mortar and pestle sign hangs above the door of the pharmacy in the foreground on the left and Stevens drapers store. During the 1920s Mr. Hood decided that he wanted to move his business to Talbot Street...

Mr. Hood, instead of finding new premises, decided to move his existing ones. On a quiet Sunday morning he nailed wooden battens over the windows and jacked up the wood built studio and darkroom by placing wooden rollers under them. Then he supervised as three sturdy Clydesdale horses were harnessed to the side of the building and inch by inch they pulled it slowly and carefully to its new site in Talbot Street.

Lumley Street looking to the north and towards Charing Cross, nowadays named La Porte Precinct to mark Grangemouth's twinning with the seaport of that name in Alabama, USA. The traditional buildings seen here have mainly been replaced with modern blocks of shops. The cobbled street surface in the foreground is made up of setts or causies, as they are often known in Scotland, and was laid in September 1906 at a cost of £1,170. It replaced the original street surface which was made up of small pieces of flint or whinstones bound together with clay and which was muddy in winter and very dusty during the summer months. The surface pictured here was, in its turn, replaced in 1920 with one of tarmacadam. As this was one of the first town streets to be finished in this way it attracted a huge amount of attention from other local authorities. The tall, three-storey, red sandstone built block on the right was Baltic Chambers, named after Grangemouth's shipping links with Scandinavia. It was in these Chambers that my grandfather, Bailie William Fyfe Hendrie, had his drapery business in the New Town as well as operating a similar shop and a ship's chandlers in the old one. Later the business transferred to premises on the opposite side of the street nearer to Charing Cross. Further along on that side of Lumley Street can be seen Stewart the butchers, Thomson the fishmongers and Barron the cycle agents outside which a bike is standing. Even further along was situated the ironmongers owned by James M.L. Urie and family.

A car splashing its way through the floods which frequently affected Lumley Street and other parts of Grangemouth in the days before the creation of the Grange Burn flood relief scheme.

This is how La Porte Precinct, formerly Lumley Street, now appears looking in the same direction as the previous photograph. (Arthur Down)

Looking in the opposite direction to the south, the changes are even more marked with the entire frontage of the street replaced by this block of modern shops. On the corner the entrance to York Arcade leading to York Square can be seen. (Arthur Down)

The courtyard of York Square looking west towards the post office. (Arthur Down)

Grangemouth's modern post office premises in York Square that replaced the previous post office in Albert Place, named after Queen Victoria's German consort. (Arthur Down)

This attractive feature in York Square was made to a design by world-famous Grangemouth modern artist Alan Davie, whose father was Principal Teacher of Art at Grangemouth High School. In November 2000, Davie, incidentally also a fine jazz saxophone player, was honoured with a retrospective exhibition at the new National Gallery of Modern Art in Dean House in Edinburgh's Belford Road. (Arthur Down)

Long before the construction of York Square, the heart of Grangemouth New Town was Charing Cross. Only two cyclists, a car and a bus comprise the traffic on this picture postcard. Looking up Station Brae, the offices of shipping agents Walter Bain and Buchan & Hogg can be seen. Also the shops occupied by Hansen's the drapers and outfitters, Knutsen the ship's chandlers and further up the hill, the other ship's chandlers owned by Christensen & Syesen Ltd, all names emphasising Grangemouth's close trading links with Scandinavia.

Charing Cross at the Millennium with modern blocks of flats rising behind the old, copper domed bank building. The weather vane on top of the spire of the bank building is, very appropriately, a sailing ship. (Arthur Down)

Looking in the opposite direction east towards Bo'ness Road, the view from Charing Cross on a wintry day in the 1920s. Apart from the messenger boy pushing a hand cart, the only other traffic is the motor bus which stood on the left hand side of the street, probably about to depart on a service run to Bo'ness five miles further down the River Forth. Charing Cross Church is on the right.

Directly opposite Charing Cross Church, Grangemouth Town Hall has changed little since pre-Second World War years, apart from the addition of wings on either side of its impressive facade to house the Lesser Town Hall and modern cloakroom facilities. The Town Hall is the second the town has possessed, the former being in the Old Town. The Earl of Zetland laid the foundation stone of the building on Saturday 27 August 1884 on a site provided by Grangemouth's chief magistrate, Bailie McPherson. Extra land was acquired from the Caledonian Railway Co. The hall can be seen with its original wrought iron railings and its decorative street lamps.

Bo'ness Road looking west towards Charing Cross and Albert Place in the 1930s. Beyond Charing Cross Church is the two-storey building that formerly housed Galloway's very popular bakery and restaurant. This well-known Grangemouth business dated back to 1906 and began in the Old Town before moving to this site at Charing Cross. The shop opened in 1926, together with the bakery that supplied it, on the site of what became the Imperial Hall but is now Zeneca House, the home of Grangemouth Heritage Trust. The enterprising Galloway family later opened another bakery in Falkirk with shop premises at 45 Vicar Street and subsequently at Bonnybridge Toll. In 1939 the firm took over the rival Tennant's Bakery in Kerse Road along with its shops in the same road and in Lumley Street. Throughout this period the Galloway brothers' bakery products won many gold medals in British national competitions. The firm received an additional boost at the start of the Second World War when the influx of RAF servicemen to the local aerodrome increased the demand for a restaurant where they could relax when off duty. The Galloway family seized this opportunity by developing their restaurant above their shop that offered splendid views of all that was happening in the heart of the town. The younger son of the Galloway family, Wilson, also did his war service in the RAF and, when demobbed in 1946, returned to run the business with his brother. Despite shortages and rationing they continued to develop the business. In 1955 Galloway's was among the first premises in the New Town to apply for a license and was finally granted one at the third application in 1956. This enabled the restaurant to serve drinks with meals from 10.30 a.m. until 2 p.m. and from 5 p.m. until 9 p.m. in winter and until 9.30 p.m. in summer. On 22 December 1962, Galloway's suffered a severe set back when, in the middle of the night, it was gutted by fire. It soon re-opened in temporary premises erected in the car park and the restaurant was back in business by June. At its busiest Galloway's employed seventy-five staff. However, in 1972 it was decided to restrict production to supplying its own restaurant and the Bo'ness Road shop with a subsequent reduction in employees to seventeen. In 1985, Dryburgh Brewers bought the business and proceeded to close it, while Wilson and his wife, Betty, have enjoyed their retirement in the town.

Charing Cross as it is today looking towards La Porte Precinct. The building on the corner houses the Royal Bank of Scotland with the offices of solicitors Tait & Mackenzie above it. The senior partner, John Kenny, is well known world-wide as a director of the Rotary movement. (Arthur Down)

Attractive tree-lined Bo'ness Road, with its substantial houses, was always the main thoroughfare in Grangemouth New Town, shown here in the 1920s before it was tarmacadamed.

Inch House, on the south side of Bo'ness Road, was originally a farm belonging to the Dundas Estate. It took its name from the Gaelic for an island and this is a reminder of how pancake flat and prone to flooding the countryside around Grangemouth was. With its ivy covered walls, its front porch and its immaculately clipped conifers the Inch was also my family home. I remember many details of it well – from the stone flagged dairy to the large kitchen and the spacious gas-lit living rooms. The original farm cottages still stood behind it and beyond them in Ronaldshay Crescent were situated the premises of joiner Arthur Lawson. Adam Sands, always known as Adie, operated a second joiners business in the Inch Yard. Inch House was ultimately demolished to make way for a petrol station. Now things have come full circle and it is expected to be replaced with seven new houses, so hopefully the old name will be revived.

Though the old Inch was knocked down, the detached villas opposite it on the north side of Bo'ness Road still survive with little altered. (Arthur Down)

Another of the Victorian villas to survive on Bo'ness Road now houses the town's popular Lea Park Hotel whose proprietor is seen chatting with the author. When it first opened in 1955 Leapark was the first business in Grangemouth to obtain a drinks license, followed shortly afterwards by the new Ellwyn Restaurant in Newlands Road. The house that was converted into Lea Park's reception hall and dining room was previously the home of Mr Miller of Grangemouth Dockyard Co. (Arthur Down)

Lea Park Hotel also took over this neighbouring house to which it is connected by a modern link block. This new block housed the hotel's ballroom and was the popular setting for many wedding receptions. It is now the hotel's busy bar restaurant and additional conference rooms have been added including the Garden Suite whose entrance is on the right. (Arthur Down)

Attractive little St Mary's Church with its steeply-raked, slate roof is home to Grangemouth's Scottish Episcopalian congregation who share their priest with the congregation of St Catherine's, Bo'ness. St Mary's stands on the corner of Ronaldshay Crescent, another local place name derived from the Dundas family's connections with the Northern Isles of Scotland. (Arthur Down)

Victoria Road with its bungalows and blocks of flats is one of Grangemouth's pleasant residential streets, September 2000. (Arthur Down)

Abbots Road during the 1920s. The house on the right is Abbotsleigh. Notice the little boy and girl walking along the bank of the Grange Burn.

The popular premises of the YMCA used to stand on the west side of Abbots Road and were the scene of a great deal of the town's youth activities from badminton matches to popular weekend dances. During the Second World War, it housed a canteen for local servicemen, especially from the aerodrome!

Moving further south along Abbots Road, Kerse Church, with its unusual spire, still stands, but is depicted without the hall that was added later. It was photographed from Zetland Park whose famous fountain can also be seen on its original site. It has subsequently been moved several times but still survives as an attractive feature of the park.

Looking north along the length of Abbots Road on the left and Park Road on the right, the former red sandstone buildings of the Grange School can be seen.

The buildings of the Grange School have been demolished and in their place stand two blocks of attractive modern flats named Brown Court after a local Grangemouth town councillor. To avoid confusion residents wished separate names for the different blocks including the much more attractive Zetland View. (Arthur Down)

While the Grange School has disappeared, opposite the two three-storey apartment blocks that replaced it, the beautifully designed Church of St Francis still stands. This is where the town's Roman Catholic population worships. With its high pitched roof covered in red tiles and its pillared entrance, it is one of the most attractive Catholic churches in Scotland. The simple beauty found inside complements its stylish exterior. A second Catholic church, Christ the King, serves the Bowhouse area of the town. (Arthur Down)

Four

Grangemouth at Work

With its excellent port facilities and the abundance of flat ground which aided road and rail links, Grangemouth prospered more and more throughout the nineteenth century as an industrial location. It is known that there was a pottery and a salt works in the area previously but it was only after the opening of the Forth & Clyde Canal and the growth of the docks that the town became a highly desirable site for new developments.

As early as 1784 there is mention of a whale oil refinery near the Grange Burn. Two years later its owner Henry Swinton also opened a fish-curing factory to salt the 'wee garvies', the little herring which were caught out in the Forth, and export them, packed in barrels, to the Scandinavian countries which lacked the coal to fuel salt pans of their own.

Shipbuilding was first undertaken in Grangemouth by Alexander Hart and continued for over two centuries. Many of the early enterprises served the needs of the ships that visited the port, for example, Walter McTarget's rope works in Dalgrain Road and later also on the west side of the Carron Wharf. Also the block makers operated by John Laird to make the wooden apparatus required to hoist sails, many of which were manufactured in the town by the McTargets in a loft in one of the five local granaries.

The granaries were designed to store imported grain, but were also used to store many other cargoes ranging from paint to brandy and other spirits. One of the granaries, built in 1811, survived in Carron Street until it was demolished in 1966 and another utilised by Carron Company to store the castings it exported was still in use as a store up until the closure of the Dockyard Co.

Another trade with an equally long connection with the town and which still provides much employment is the import of timber. Famous names associated with it include Christie & Vesey, Brownlee, Muirhead and MacPherson & McLaren. By 1906 Grangemouth had forty-five acres of timber basins designed for the storing and seasoning of Baltic pitch pine logs and there were also several pit prop yards busy in the town.

Grangemouth's connection with the chemical and oil industries for which it is now so famous began with opening of the Scottish Co-operative Wholesale Society's Soap Works in 1897. This continued in 1906 when the Anglo-American Oil Co. chose the port as the site to erect the first ever oil-storage tanks in Scotland. Scottish Dyes Ltd, the predecessor of ICI and all the companies that followed it, first came to the town in 1919, immediately after the First World War. Scottish Oils Ltd began the oil refinery in 1924 but lack of supplies forced the refinery to close during the Second World War. However, in the late 1940s it expanded rapidly again to earn for Grangemouth the title of 'Scotland's Boom Town'.

Sir William Fraser showed Her Majesty Queen Elizabeth, now the Queen Mother, around the oil refinery during a royal visit to the site in 1950s. On the right the works' foreman Tommy Thomson can be seen.

At the start of the big day, Her Majesty was welcomed to Grangemouth by the Lord Lieutenant of Stirlingshire, Sir Ian Bolton, while the town's proud Provost, John Binnie, stood waiting to receive her in front of BP's headquarters. Behind him on the steps stood Sir William and Lady Fraser while the posse of press cameramen captured the moment for posterity.

Before entering the offices Her Majesty paused to chat with Sir William, who was Chairman of the Anglo-Iranian Oil Co., the forerunner of BP. Provost John Binnie is seen on the steps.

Later during the royal visit Sir William escorted Her Majesty aboard the oil tanker, *British Genius* which was berthed in the docks. Here they are seen with Jetty Superintendent, John Syme, in his trench coat, while Provost John Binnie and Lady Fraser followed behind them.

Grangemouth's famous aerodrome used to be situated directly opposite the oil refinery. Its impressive aircraft hangars and central passenger terminal and control tower are seen to advantage from the air on the day of its opening in 1939. The timing of that date was, of course, a most unfortunate one as the declaration of war on Sunday 3 September completely altered the future of what should have been one of the town's most successful ventures. The story of Central Scotland Airport as it was to be known, began in February 1939 with the publication of an advert in the *Scotsman*. This read:

> *Acting on the recommendations of the Maybury Report that there should be a central airport for Scotland midway between Glasgow and Edinburgh, Scottish Aviation Ltd have made arrangements to take over a tract of 550 acres adjoining the south east corner of Grangemouth. Investigations have proved the countryside surrounding both Edinburgh and Glasgow could not provide individual airports of the required standard in close proximity. Grangemouth it is believed provides the ideal solution to a big problem. One of the most remarkable features of this mammoth airport is the fact that contractors have guaranteed to complete the job within three months. Work will commence of Monday 6 February and the aerodrome will be opened on 1 May.*

The exact moment of the official opening of Grangemouth Aerodrome was caught on film as Air Marshall Viscount Trenchard started the propeller of a model Spitfire set on a cigar box. This triggered the release of a smoke bomb on the grass in front of the terminal's passenger lounge. The invited guests could watch the ceremony through the large plate glass windows. As the smoke cleared, the excited spectators saw a whole flight of nine Hawker-Hart aircraft flying in formation overhead before coming in to land on the aerodrome's grass runway. That the runway was grass surfaced was the secret of how it had been possible to open the airport in such a remarkably short time. At the time it was the best and largest facility of its kind in Scotland and passenger flights to London began early the following Monday morning.

Central Scotland Airport never gained the distinction of providing scheduled international flights, but the largest plane which took part in its official opening was this impressive silver painted Dakota belonging to Royal Dutch Airlines, KLM, and the company's representative announced proudly that it intended to introduce regular flights to Amsterdam. Sadly the Second World War intervened and while Grangemouth did magnificent service as a RAF fighter station and later as an equally successful training base, by the time the hostilities were over ideas had changed and separate airports were developed for Edinburgh at Turnhouse and for Glasgow at Renfrew. The opportunity to centralise all Scottish services had been lost and any chance that Grangemouth might attract back some passenger flights was finally destroyed by the expansion soon afterwards of the adjoining oil refinery.

This steam-powered crane used to operate at SCWS's Grangemouth Soap Works that was the largest plant of its kind in Scotland and one of the largest in Britain. The raw materials required to produce the soap were stored in the large shed on the left and were all imported through the docks. The word 'glycerine' appears on the front of the factory as this was a by-product of the soap making process. The manager for many years was Cllr Joe Penny who later became

The two main brands made at the SCWS Soap Works in Grangemouth were White Windsor and Lovely and here local women are seen packing the bars of soap. The Soap Works was the first in the area to employ women. The demand for bars of soap decreased during the 1950s because of the introduction of powdered detergents and this, combined with the advertisements of major rivals on commercial television, which came to Scotland in 1956, finally led to the closure of the factory in 1966.

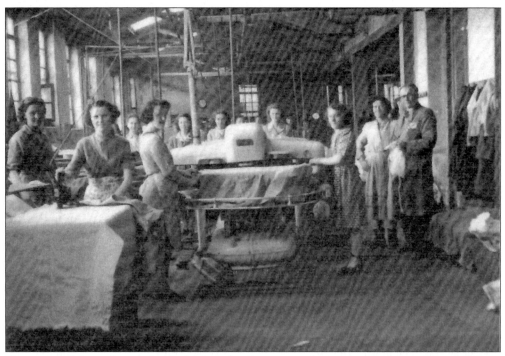

Grangemouth Laundry, run by the Murray family, was another major employer of female labour in the town.

The operators at Grangemouth's manual telephone exchange were also all local women including Ina Drummond, now Mrs Fairley, who still lives in the town. In the days before it was finally automated with the arrival of STD (Subscriber Trunk Dialling) it is said that local football fans unable to attend a match used to telephone the operators at half and full time to check the scores at local games.

The workers at MacPherson & McLaren's posed with their massive circular saw blades and large cross saws at the Grangemouth sawmill. Notice how young some of the apprentices looked in the days when boys could still leave school at the age of twelve. Later the leaving age was increased to fourteen, and then fifteen but it did not become the present sixteen until the 1960s. Several of the men and boys pictured here later signed this picture.

The workforce at Muirhead's Sawmill.

Aerial view publicity postcard by the management at Muirhead's Sawmill. The extensive size of the timber basin, where the wood was seasoned, is clearly illustrated. Muirhead's pioneered the use of pre-laminated timber and supplied the materials for the famous Crown of Thorns, which adorns the old stone steeple of St Michael's Kirk in nearby Linlithgow. Its former managing director, Jack Lindsay, aged ninety-two, still lives in the district.

Here two of Muirhead's employees are seen at work on the shop floor.

The tall chimney at Jinkabout Mill as seen on the road to Polmont. The mill took its name from the fact that it was situated at a bend in the River Avon. At one time Dr John Roebuck and the Cadell brothers considered the site when trying to find the right place for their iron works that were finally built on the shores of the Carron.

Farming was also an important source of labour in the countryside around Grangemouth. This picture shows the attractive farmhouse at Bowhouse, after which the modern primary school is named. Many of the town's farms were destroyed in 1939 during the construction of the aerodrome including Abbotsgrange, Claret, Dalgleish's, Reddoch and Roy's Reddoch. Others had been swallowed up even earlier when they were acquired in 1924 by Scottish Oils to make room for the oil refinery. This now stands on the lands of Easter, Mid and West Saltcoats with the earliest refinery buildings on the eastern side of the road from Bo'ness Road to Powdrake. In 1952 the acreage of the refinery was increased vastly by the acquisition of even more good farm land when Bearcroft, Oldwells, Ten acres and what remained of Claret were all taken over.

Near the Bowhouse Plank, a plank of wood by which local people crossed the Grange Burn before a proper bridge was erected making access to the farm cottages in the background more convenient. The long, low line of farm workers' homes was later demolished to make way for modern housing developments.

The lands of other Grangemouth farms were bought over for house building including the fields of Newhouse Farm whose fine farmhouse is seen in this photo.

Another of Grangemouth's former farms.

On the banks of the Grange Burn looking south, past the bridge across Bo'ness Road to the spire of the Grange Church on the corner of Park Road and Ronaldshay Crescent. It was originally published as a local Christmas card and sold by Grangemouth newsagents around the time of the First World War.

Many Grangemouth men fought and died in the First World War, supposedly 'the war to end all wars.' The war memorial erected after at the entrance to the Zetland Park caused great controversy because instead of being a simple obelisk or figure of a soldier, it showed the British lion crushing the German eagle.

Sadly the First World War did not 'end all wars'. Members of the Grangemouth Air Raid Patrol are seen parading past the War Memorial on an Armistice Sunday during the Second World War. Those of the ARP with bicycles acted as messengers in addition to their duties. They ensured that the blackout precautions were strictly enforced to avoid enemy bombing raids on the town and were engaged in spotting and extinguishing any fires should an attack take place.

The men of the Grangemouth part-time volunteer fire brigade posed with their young mascot outside the Municipal Chambers in Bo'ness Road. The little boy is Duncan Bryce, whose father was one of the fire fighters. (Isabel McNab)

Officials of Grangemouth Co-operative Society outside the society's registered office in Lumley Street beside the ambulance its members helped to buy to help the war effort.

The manager of Grangemouth Co-operative Society's grocery department comes to the door with his white apron-clad assistants to pose.

For its many members the Co-op or the Store as it was known was far more than simply a place to shop. The Co-operative movement was very much a way of life in which they actively participated as members. The level of their purchases dictated the amount of quarterly dividend they received. As well as running a large range of shops, from grocery stores, butchers and bakers to a drapery department, the Co-op also operated a hairdressing saloon. The six assistants from the drapery posed. Interestingly the smallest of them is also the smallest of the Brownies seen in a photo taken ten years earlier in front of the Town Hall which appears later in this book.

Staff from one of the busiest departments at Grangemouth Co-op, the bakery. The horse drawn carts that also brought the morning milk delivered the morning rolls that they produced. Later in the day the same bakers' vans also went round the streets of the town selling bread and teabreads. These included pancakes, scones, plain cookies, iced cookies and most popular of all – cream cookies – together with many kinds of cakes all of which were produced in the local bakery.

Grangemouth Co-op Bakery did not have a monopoly however, because the bread and cakes produced by John Tennant also had many loyal customers. Here Mr Tennant is pictured with one of his young delivery boys carrying the wicker basket used to move items from the van to customers' doors. Notice the larger wicker hamper on the roof of this Dad's Army type motor van. With its open compartment for the driver who had to brave the elements come summer or winter as he made his daily rounds of the streets of the town. One of Tennant's apprentices was a young man called John Galloway who went on to open his own bakery and in 1939 took over the firm with which he had served his time and learned his trade.

Another of Mr. Tennant's fellow shopkeepers in Grangemouth was local butcher Alexander Stewart. One of his staff appears to have been called up into the forces at the time this photo was taken.

J. Lindsay, Fishmongers, had their premises in Kings Road round the corner from Bo'ness Road. They purchased their fish fresh daily from the markets at Granton and Newhaven and many Grangemouth families enjoyed their fired haddock as a tasty tea time treat and was always considered superior to cod or, worse still, whiting.

Did Lindsay the fishmonger ever sell salmon? If so it may well have been caught locally at nearby Dunmore. The tiny, mud-silted harbour can be seen with the smoking chimneys of Grangemouth oil refinery visible further down the River Forth. The Dunmore fishermen used the unusual method of half-net fishing to catch the salmon, some of which was dispatched to Billingsgate Market in London to obtain the best prices. Since the late 1970s more salmon have returned to the Forth, as efforts to decrease pollution of its waters are slowly proving successful. The building beyond the pier is the village blacksmith's and the doorway is appropriately designed in the shape of a horseshoe. (John Doherty)

Grangemouth officials during the Water Board outing in 1950. Grangemouth formerly had its own water board whose members ensured that the town had an excellent clean supply.

In the 1920s a steam-powered lorry proved too heavy for one of Grangemouth's wooden bascule bridges which spanned the Forth & Clyde Canal.

One of the earliest mentions of policing in Grangemouth occurred in March 1858 when control of the local police was transferred away from the local superiors, the Dundas family. As happened everywhere in Scotland it switched to that of the Commissioners of Supply, early forerunners of County Councillors. In December 1872 Grangemouth became a Police Burgh meaning its policemen were controlled by newly appointed local Police Commissioners who later became Town Councillors. The police station originally overlooked the Junction Lock on the Forth & Clyde Canal in the Old Town. In 1961 the police station moved to its present site beside the Municipal Chambers in Bo'ness Road. By this date the local force had grown in strength to one Chief Inspector, one Inspector, five Sergeants, twenty-four Constables and two femal police officers. This police car was pictured in Moray Place. (Arthur Down)

As a prosperous port, Grangemouth had branches of all the major Scottish Banks including the British Linen, whose impressive red sandstone offices still stand in La Porte Percent, formerly Lumley Street, but are now the offices of solicitors and estate agents, Marshall & Wilson. On the first floor there is a dental surgery. (Arthur Down)

The old toll-house at the bridge over the River Avon shortly before demolition. This was where travellers had to pay their dues when journeying between Grangemouth and Bo'ness. Standing in the shadow of the oil refinery's distinctive cooling towers it survived until the late 1970s. Notice that the windows jutted out to make it easier for the toll keeper to spot approaching vehicles and to collect the dues.

Five

Grangemouth at School

The first written record of education in Grangemouth occurred in 1789 when mention was made of a schoolmistress teaching classes in the town. She was succeeded by Grangemouth's first Dominie, George Ritchie, who was provided with a salary of £12 by Lord Dundas, to be supplemented by the fees that he collected from his pupils. When Ritchie died in 1806 a second Dominie, James Sinclair, was appointed in his place.

Twenty years later, in 1827, a report recorded that, 'Grangemouth is well provided with means of education. There has been erected by Lady Dundas an elegant building containing a schoolroom for boys and another for girls, an ante-room which is used as a library and dwelling houses for teachers.' By 1836 secondary education was available in the town, for those who could afford the fees, at what was described as Grangemouth Academy. However, there was no direct connection between this establishment and the more familiar building built as the High School in 1909 of which so many Portonians have fond schoolday memories.

In 1851 Zetland Primary School had a roll of 170 pupils and two decades later, when primary education in Scotland became compulsory, this figure rose to 204. Although law now enforced attendance from the age of five to twelve, fees still had to be paid and were not abolished until 1891. Also in this year the feu on the east shore of the Grange Burn was acquired upon which the Grange School was erected to provide secondary education in the town. It admitted its first pupils in 1893, although it was not officially opened until the following year.

In 1900 the School Boards of Polmont, Bothkennar and Grangemouth were combined as the Grangemouth Parish School Board and two members from it were delegated to visit each school. The exception was the town's new Roman Catholic primary that opened in 1901 as it was under the separate control of the church.

In 1909 the new Grangemouth Academy was completed. As was traditional in most Scottish towns it accepted both boys and girls, but in other respects educational provision differed in Grangemouth. Following the mixed infant school, boys and girls were separated for the remainder of their primary years, boys going to Dundas school and girls to the Grange.

Half a century later Grangemouth was the scene of another unusual educational experiment. Grangemouth became the only place in Scotland with a three-tier educational system. When the new High School in Tinto Drive opened, the original High School building was converted into Abbotsgrange Middle School while Moray Junior Secondary was similarly changed.

The Grange School, on the banks of the Grange Burn, was a familiar Grangemouth landmark. Its most famous headmaster was Charles W. Thomson, MA. In 1901, at twenty-nine, he was appointed over forty-seven other candidates. He soon proved that although he had taught for the previous three years in Hutchesons' Girl's Grammar School, Glasgow, he was no soft mark. In his memoirs he notes:

> *At three epochs in my forty years experience I found the tawse a very helpful adjunct to other disciplinary measures. The second of these periods when I used the tawse freely was at the beginning of my first head-ship at Grangemouth where the School Board told me my first task was to kill truancy which had been averaging fifteen cases a day. I intimated a definite tariff for truancy of so many palmies for a whole day and a similar proportionate number for a half day or for several days even although the total exceeded the strokes in the Board's corporal punishment regulations displayed on the classroom walls. My leather strap weighed only three ounces, far lighter than the dreaded 'Lochgelly Special', but news of the increased number of licks for which miscreants were guaranteed to have to keep their hands held out spread throughout the school and this together with my rule that all lessons missed must be made up after four o'clock soon improved attendance! This problem solved, my work at Grangemouth became most congenial and the convenor of the School Board who was a local butcher was the most helpful I ever encountered. The school's strengths were the teaching of commercial subjects, much appreciated by local businessmen and instruction in German, which proved useful in the work of the port.*

Grange School as seen from neighbouring Zetland Park. After Mr Thomson was promoted to Rector of Larkhall Academy, the Grange became an all-girl's school and its last headmistress, during the half century it fulfilled this role, was the well-remembered Miss Peggy Urie. Her family was well known in the town as the owners of the local ironmongers. After her retirement the Grange became a mixed primary school until its final closure. It was then demolished and replaced by the blocks of modern flats that now occupy the site.

At the start of the 1900s this class of pupils posed with their teacher for this school photograph. The little girl in white in the middle of the second row from the front is my aunt, Maude.

The solid stone-built Dundas Primary School catered only for boys as this class photograph from the 1920s shows. The three lads seated in the front row are sitting on a coconut-hair gym mat. Shorts made from grey flannel were the usual school wear at this time and seem to have been worn by most of the boys in the picture. Being an all boys' school, Dundas had a reputation for strict discipline, which was probably necessary judging from the size of this class that numbered over forty lively boys.

The Infant School, 1920, with a class lined up in the playground, looks stern and formal. The long narrow classroom windows were designed specifically to allow daylight in, but to prevent pupils wasting time by looking out.

The Infant School class with their teacher, Miss Hopkin, whose family owned the shipping company of Hopkin & Paton.

The girls of the Grange School.

The original Grangemouth High School building was officially opened in 1909. It served the town well until the 1960s when larger premises at Bowhouse replaced it. With the opening of the new High School buildings with their better playing field facilities, the building became one of the town's two Middle Schools. Under the name of Abbotsgrange Middle School it catered for half of the town's ten to thirteen year olds in what would otherwise have been the top two primary and lowest two secondary classes. The Middle School experiment was the idea of Stirlingshire Director of Education Mr H. Meldrum, who championed it enthusiastically, but it did not prove sufficiently attractive to be adopted anywhere else in Scotland. As pupil numbers in the town dropped during the 1980s it was decided by the local education authority to revert to the normal pattern of primary and secondary schools.

A class of girls wearing gymslips and neatly dressed boys at Grangemouth High School during the 1930s. Mr Auchinachy the Headmaster is seen standing in the centre. The teacher on the left was Head of Science, Mr McClemont, and on the right is Principal Teacher of Mathematics, John Maxwell. Mr Maxwell was better known by his nickname, Pongo, which the dictionary defines as a young soldier returned from battle, which described him exactly when he joined the staff after the First World War.

Headmaster of Grangemouth High School, Mr Auchinachy, in front of the school building with his staff. Back row: -?-, Mr McClemont (Principal Teacher of Science), 'Nunkie' Davie (Principal Teacher of Art), Mr John Maxwell (Principal Teacher of Mathematics), -?-, -?- . Middle row: Miss McEwan, -?-, Miss Urwin, -?-, -?-, Miss Minty, Miss Nicol, Mr Ripley (janitor). Front row: -?-, Miss McKay, Mr Auchinachy, -?-, Miss Riddick.

In 1938 the High School organised a visit to France and these smiling girls, with their new-found French friends, were amongst the pupils who enjoyed the visit to St Servans near St Malo, Brittany. The Grangemouth girls in the picture include Marjory Wood, Maude Maxwell, Roma Stewart and Nancy Whitehead.

The Grangemouth High School pupils pose in the cobbled street outside a souvenir shop with their French friends. It was hoped that the visit would develop into an ongoing exchange between the two towns, but only a year later the outbreak of the Second World War put paid to this idea. Despite the following years of enemy occupation, some of the pupils managed to stay in touch and corresponded for many years.

Grangemouth High School pupils, 1948, posed in front of the main entrance for this class photograph.

Grangemouth High School's modern premises at Bowhouse pictured shortly after the start of the new school year in September 2000. (Arthur Down)

After years as an experimental middle school, the Moray School has reverted to being a primary catering for pupils from four to twelve. (Arthur Down)

Six

Civic and Social Life in Grangemouth

Grangemouth has always been a town where people have worked and played hard. It has also been well provided with a wide range of sports clubs and activities together with one of the finest public parks in Scotland. The park was gifted to the town in 1880 by the Earl of Zetland, whose name it bears, and was officially opened on Saturday 3 June 1882. The turning on of the fountain erected by the town's chief magistrate, timber merchant Bailie McPherson, marked the occasion. He hoped that it would not only be decorative but useful to the many visitors that the park would attract. Features of the park included a typically Victorian bandstand where Zetland Brass Band performed summer concerts and two football pitches.

The park was extended by another twenty-five acres during the 1920s, nineteen of them from Blair Drummond Estate, including what became one of its most popular attractions – The Orchard. Other attractions included its open-air swimming pool and a large paddling and boating pool for children.

In 1953 the park was enlarged again with the addition of a further seventeen acres creating a total of fifty-one acres for public enjoyment. Since then Grangemouth has continued to keep pace with modern developments in the provision of recreational facilities with the building of an indoor swimming pool and recreation centre on the banks of the Grange Burn and the opening of the town's magnificent sports stadium. The original cost of this first class athletics venue was £72,000 and it can accommodate 15,000 spectators with seating for 2,000 in the grandstand. Its 440-yard, five-lane running track was the first all-weather track in Scotland and was provided with a rubberised asphalt surface. Events held at the stadium have ranged from highland games to the annual Scottish Schools Road Race.

The first occasion on which Grangemouth Children's Day was held in its present form – with a schoolgirl Queen – was on Friday 17 August 1906 when the coronation of Nancy Peddie took place. The man behind the creation of the Children's Day, which is still a highlight of the town's summer, was my grandfather Bailie William Fyfe Hendrie. This picture shows the bower girls and ladies-in-waiting that made up Queen Nancy's royal retinue on that warm summer day almost a century ago.

Appropriately Bailie Hendrie's youngest son, Nelson Patrick (on the left), who was my father, played the part of one of the two pageboys who served Queen Nancy. Here the two pages are seen in their white uniforms with tricorn hats.

A Children's Day procession making its way along Kerse Road to the crowning ceremony in the Zetland Park shortly before the outbreak of the First World War. The hostilities disrupted the Children's Day festivities for several years.

By the 1920s the Children's Day festivities were back in full swing.

The crowd gathers to watch an early Children's Day procession.

Fashionably cloch-hatted teachers accompanied the children in this Children's Day procession during the 1920s. The weather was not very favourable as the flags billowed in a stiff breeze. In the background can be seen the bascule bridge over the Forth & Clyde Canal which carried the road between the Old and New Towns.

A Children's Day parade during the 1930s, making its way down Station Brae to Charing Cross. The tall factory chimney of McPherson McLaren's timber mill looms in the background.

In the New Town the Children's Day procession passed along Kerse Road. Here the schoolgirls with their ribbon adorned straw boaters and white gala day dresses and the boys with their caps in their school colours are seen passing G. Rigreazzi's popular refreshment rooms which sold excellent Italian ice cream. Next door was the dairy belonging to the well-known Neville family, which also sold home-made ice cream as well as cheese, butter and milk.

Every Grangemouth May Day culminated in sports in the Zetland Park where this large group of children and adults posed for the photographer.

Decorative house fronts are now a popular feature at modern Children's Days, but in the past the main emphasis was on the creation of triumphal arches. Built of a timber frame covered in clipped, green boxwood it was erected in 1926, the year of the General Strike, and its proud designers and builders pose below it. Notice the baby being held high in the centre of the picture while a dog saunters across the road in front of the assembled men.

The fountain that Bailie McLaren gifted to Grangemouth to mark the opening of the Zetland Park in 1882 is still a feature well over a century later. In the background is the bowling pavilion. (Arthur Down)

While the fountain and pavilion have survived, the ornate wrought iron bandstand where the Zetland Brass Band used to play its summer concerts was demolished and sold to a small town in the USA and re-erected.

While Grangemouth managed to stage its Children's Day celebrations in 1926, despite the economic depression and the resultant industrial unrest in the country, the Second World War forced the abandonment of the festivities until peace returned in 1945. In 1946 the first post-war gala took place when Sacred Heart Primary School pupil, Sarah McAllister, was crowned May Day Queen even though the ceremony was actually performed on a Saturday in June as it always is nowadays. Mrs J. Henery performed the coronation ceremony on the stage in the Zetland Park.

Another attraction during bygone summers in Grangemouth were the town's popular swimming galas. Here the crowd lined Basin Street to watch the fun.

Here a competitor is seen walking the greasy pole, an event that called for a great deal of nimbleness. It always delighted the large crowd of spectators who came to watch the fun and revel in the competitors losing their balance and falling into the water.

By the 1920s Grangemouth had acquired a proper open-air swimming pool in the Zetland Park. During its first season, however, enthusiastic swimmers had to make do with temporary railway carriage changing rooms.

The completed pool that was situated to the east of where the present indoor pool stands.

A swimming gala at the new open air pool in Zetland park. The trophies that were being competed for can be seen on the table on the poolside in front of the officials.

The opening of the outdoor pool gave a considerable boost to the membership of Grangemouth Swimming Club. The participants pose with their coaches for the team photograph taken in front of the flagstaff in the Zetland Park. The fine stone built houses in Drummond Place can be glimpsed behind them.

The great popularity of swimming in Grangemouth is confirmed yet again by these boys diving into the waters of the Grange Burn during the 1920s. Some of the town's first council-built houses can be seen in the background. It is interesting to note the style of swimming costumes worn by the boys and to wonder if summers were generally warmer in these days gone by.

Swimwear fashions changed as evidenced by these young swimmers at the outdoor pool in the Zetland Park.

This informal group photograph was taken during one of the final seasons at the outdoor swimming pool in the Zetland Park. The open-air pool was filled in after the completion of the town's modern indoor swimming pool on Abbots Road.

Grangemouth's many stretches of open water from the timber basins to the Grange Burn and from the docks to the canal always attracted lots of hungry swans and feeding them was another popular summer pastime. In the past, Grangemouth was often known as Scotland's 'Little Holland'.

This small putting course was set up behind Stanner's hairdressers. To modern eyes the boys in their school caps and uniforms in the foreground and the girls with their blazers in the background all seem very formally dressed to be indulging in such an activity.

A piper led these participants in the ICI Gala sports.

Muirhead's Pipe Band brought Grangemouth wide-spread publicity when they became World Champions.

Grangemouth was famous for its pipe bands and this picture shows the town's juvenile band with their tutor, Mr J. Burns, who was also the local cobbler. Backrow, left to right: J. Reid, J. Bell. Third row: J. McLeod, C. Martin, A. Scotland, B. Jack, J. McPhail. First row: D. Marmion, A. Downie, J. Owens, J. Campbell, J. Todd and J. Boyd. Front row: J. Grossart and J. Reid.

For many years Grangemouth loyally supported two junior football teams. The 1924 Forth Rangers team is pictured in their distinctive striped shirts. They played in the Old Town and their Clyde Street pitch was often flooded by the tides.

Forth Rangers rivals, Grange Rovers, during the 1923/24 season. Their Wood Street ground stood beyond Alexander's bus depot.

The runners of Grangemouth Harriers in 1920 with their team coach.

Grangemouth also had its own cricket team. Their ground was near the SCWS Soap Works and here the players are seen posing in their whites and blazers in front of their wooden pavilion with its white picket fence.

Grangemouth bowlers posed with the trophies won during the season. The house in the background is Inch Cottage.

Grangemouth Girl Guides and Brownies on the steps in front of the new Grangemouth Town Hall at Charing Cross. From oldest to youngest the girls all wore similar pudding basin hats, but the colour of their tunics varied from the royal blue of the older guides at the back to the brown of the little Brownies at the front. Notice also the four guide leaders, two on either side of the group. Try to spot the smallest Brownie who grew up to become an assistant in the drapery department at the Co-operative store.

The Guides in Grangemouth included Kitty Comb, Helen Finnie, Rita Galashan, Helen Kay, Norma Kerr, Jean Learmond and Frances Silver. The Guider was Isobel Williamson.

The children who attended the Saturday matinee at Grangemouth's popular cinema La Scala in front of its well-known red-brick facade. Before it took the still familiar name of La Scala it was known as The Electric Picture Palace. This name is still displayed above the entrance although it is many years since films were shown as it is now a bingo hall. La Scala belongs to Caledonian Associated Cinemas.

This further group photograph shows the uniformed members of the Grangemouth branch of the Red Cross who posed for this picture with local GP, Dr Anderson, at the conclusion of one of the regular courses that he organised for them. The members are, back row left to right: E. Dempster, ? Dick, ? Oliphant, J. Alexander, A. Robertson, B. Fernie, E. Sinclair, N. Johnstone. Middle row: J. Donald, M Wood, ? Wood, ? Moyes, M. Ritchie, B. Morrison, ? Kincaid, ? Haggart, ? Armitt. Front row, ? Fiddes, ? Harrower, ? Morrison, ? Peddie, ? Kilgour, ? Lapsley.

St Andrew's Ambulance Brigade members relaxed out of uniform at their annual presentation of prizes. The awards were handed over by their guests of honour, Provost and Mrs John Binnie, who are seated on the left in the front row accompanied by Dr David Naismith and his wife, Mary.

Provost Binnie at one of the dinner dances that used to be a very popular feature of social life in the town. The other guests include the Falkirk Herald's Grangemouth correspondent, Tom MacGowran and his wife Iris. Tom married Iris Brown in 1946 shortly after he returned home from captivity. He was imprisoned upon the fall of Singapore and had spent four years in a Japanese POW camp. They set up their first home together in the flat above the Falkirk Herald and Grangemouth Advertiser Office at Charing Cross. As local reporter he coined the description 'Scotland's Boom Town' to describe Grangemouth's financial prosperity during the post-war oil bonanza. He went on to become the Managing Director of the Johnston Press, Britain's largest local newspaper group and was honoured with the OBE. Iris' services to the community, including the local Chamber of Commerce, were recognised eleven years later when she again visited Buckingham Place to be invested with the MBE. This completed a family hat-trick as her father, the editor of the *Linlithgowshire Gazette*, had also been similarly honoured. The other couple is Mr and Mrs James Leitch.

Provost John Binnie, wearing his gold chain of office, with members of Grangemouth's very active Chamber of Commerce. They include Town Clerk, Bryce Johnston, local minister, the Reverend Martin, Mr Reid, manager of ICI, Mr Peutherer, works manager of the BP Oil Refinery, and Lindsay Wood.

Prime Minister Sir Alex Douglas Hume on an official visit to Grangemouth. He is pictured here on the steps of the Town Hall after a visit to BP. He is accompanied by BP works manager, Mr Peutherer and by David Paul who was chief chemist and by engineer, John McWilliam.

Fitzcharles offered the very latest in motorbikes, but pedal cycles were also always popular in Grangemouth because the terrain of the town was so flat. Fitzcharles supplied them and also did a profitable trade repairing tyres when they were punctured. Many older Portonians also recall making regular trips to Fitzcharles premises to have their accumulator batteries charged. The diversity of the enterprising Fitzcharles family is also seen on the notice above the door of the shop that reads, 'Cycles, Gramophones and Prams repaired.'

The Fitzcharles family were the operators of Grangemouth's first motor taxi with its convertible roof and its white fire-stoned tyres. Fitzcharles have also become well known through the country for their immaculately maintained fleet of buses and were one of the first companies in Scotland to offer all-inclusive coach tours. Their popular programme of residential excursions offers a choice not just of British destinations but also overseas ones in Europe and in Southern Ireland and many local people enjoy taking part in these well-organised tours.

Alexander's Bluebird bus fleet was always a rival of Fitzcharles. Here Grangemouth Provost John Binnie and a group of Town Councillors pose in front of one of the Bluebird touring coaches built in Falkirk.

Provost John Binnie is pictured here with Bruce Peddie, Willie Murray, ? Gloag, Joe Penny, ? Hartley, -?-, -?-, and Wilf Intin, whose daughter later became head of music at Bo'ness Academy.

Former Provost Bruce Peddie with Councillors John Binnie, Joe Penny, ? Hartley, ? Gloag and Willie Murray, manager of the laundry in the town.

Grangemouth Town Council in session in the Municipal Chambers, Bo'ness Road. With the Provost are Bailie Cornwall, Bailie John Binnie and Bailie Jimmy Tennant as well as Councillors Joe Penny, Alex McCreath and Bob Brown, Wilf Intin, Eddie Gray, and Mr Smith. Town officials in the picture include, W. Bryce-Johnston, (Town Clerk), John Stewart (Burgh Chamberlain), Mr Wallace (Burgh Engineer), Mr Lamont (Town Officer), Mr Temple.

In their scarlet, ermine-trimmed robes are Provost Smith with his Bailies and Councillors. They include Dr David Naismith, Bruce Peddie, W. Bryce-Johnson (Town Clerk) wearing his wig, his assistant Eric Dean, Alex Stanners, whose family owned the tobacconist and stationers business on Station Brae, Bailie William Ure.

To the right of Provost John Binnie stands Willie Matthews, ? Chisholm, Eric Dean (Assistant Town Clerk), W. Bryce-Johnston (Town Clerk) and, wearing his overcoat, Mr. Wallace (Burgh Engineer).

On leaving office Provost John Binnie was presented with this portrait by Bailie Stanners.

Provost Binnie invested his colleague Mr Cornwall as a Bailie watched by the Provost's wife, Maude.

The retirement of John Stewart, Grangemouth's Burgh Chamberlain, was marked by this informal gathering at Lea Park Hotel.

An all-the-year-round treat in Grangemouth was the opportunity to purchase fish and chip suppers from Mrs Morrison's mobile horse-drawn chippy. Her great rival was Mr Hotchkiss whose mobile fish fryer had four wheels!

For those who wished to eat out, the Grange Dining Room was a popular choice and was owned by A. Cimson. Here the staff take a break from serving customers to pose in the doorway. The tearoom also sold a wide range of chocolates and other confectionery with Cadbury's products being advertised in the window.

Like most ports, Grangemouth has always had many pubs, but perhaps none more famous than the bar of the Queen's Hotel in the Old Town.

One of Grangemouth's modern hostelries at Charlotte Dundas Court, is the Avongrange. Well-known local licensee, Walter Gowans, who previously owned the famous Dutch Inn in the neighbouring village of Skinflats, originally started the business. The Avongrange was officially opened by popular Scottish personality, actor Jamieson Clark. (Arthur Down)

Grangemouth civic leaders were joined by their ladies when this photograph was taken. They include Nana Tennant, Alex Stanners and Maude Binnie.

During the 1950s Grangemouth was honoured by a visit from the Moderator of the Church of Scotland who was received on the steps of the Municipal Chambers in Bo'ness Road. Provost William Sharp officially opened the Municipal Chambers on 30 October 1939. The building cost £19,500, and after the end of the war an annexe was added at a further cost of £30,700. Grangemouth ceased being an independent burgh on 1 April 1975 during Scottish local government re-organisation following publication of the Wheatley Report. It became part of the Falkirk District of Central Region. In 1995 Central Region was in turn abolished and Grangemouth became part of Falkirk Unitary Authority. Community Councils have been established to allow local opinion to be expressed, but despite assurances from politicians and officials that the latest system is more efficient and economical to run, most Portonians still regret the abolition of their own Town Council. They considered the old system more immediately responsive to complaints about services and reflected better the way in which they wanted their home town to be administered.

Grangemouth High School's summer outing was always one of the highlights of the school year. Here teachers and pupils are seen relaxing while enjoying a picnic. On the right is George Maxwell, known to his pupils as 'Bud'. Next to him, seated on the grass, is Head of Art, Mr Davie, with technical teacher Mr MacKenzie seated in the centre. Principal teacher of Science, Mr McClemont, who later became headmaster of the school, is seated on the wicker hamper. Standing on the left is Mr Henderson whose nickname was 'Doo' and seated at his feet in the dark suit is Principal Teacher of Mathematics, John Maxwell who was nicknamed 'Pongo'.

The same school picnic when the 5th and 6th year girls posed with the ever-popular John Maxwell and Mr Davie who is seated in the middle of the group.

More members of the staff of Grangemouth High School are seen in relaxed mood on the steps of the front entrance to the school. They include Miss Mackay, Miss Minty, Mr McClemont, Miss White, Mr Davie, Miss Reid, Miss Fraser, Mr Maxwell, Miss Riddick and Mr Henderson.

Grangemouth High School senior pupils including, Jimmy McGibbon, Jim Marshall, Isabel Ellis, Bruce Smith, Jean Porteus, Ina Gartshore and Moira Stewart.

Back in the 1930s navy serge gymslips were standard school wear for girls, but why are six of the girls in the picture in uniform while the other girls and boys are in civvies? Those pictured in front of Grangemouth High School's red sandstone facade are Marjory Wood, Isabel Tennant, Janey Combe, Bill Telfer, Margaret Bain. Isabel Campbell, Muriel Stewart, May Intin and Margaret Peatfield. The old school building still stands, but was converted into apartment homes when staff and pupils moved to more modern accommodation at Tinto Drive, Bowhouse.

Boys seemed to outnumber girls at Grangemouth High School in the 1940s, when this photo was taken.

Teenage members of the very popular Bowhouse Community Centre table tennis club outside the building during a break from practice. The man who inspired so many youngsters, team coach Charlie Gillespie, is in front of the window in the background. At one time the club had around forty members.

The Cadger's Brae, despite its name, was one of Grangemouth's best-loved beauty spots and a favourite walk for local courting couples.

Passengers crowded the decks of the *Fair Maid* for this evening river cruise for which there was music for dancing – if there was space!

The *Fair Maid* was the most popular of the Forth pleasure steamers during the 1920s and '30s and regularly carried Portonians on summer outings to Aberdour, Kinghorn, and other seaside resorts further down the Firth of Forth. In 1866 the *Fair Maid* was launched at McKnight's Shipbuilding Yard, Ayr and began her life as a steamer on the River Clyde. She was originally named *Madge Wildfire*, after one of the characters in the novels of Sir Walter Scott. In 1906 she transferred to the Forth until 1939 when she was requisitioned by the Admiralty and unfortunately never returned from war service.

The old *Fair Maid* sailed to and from Grangemouth Docks, where this modern vessel is seen waiting to load cargo. As she is 'light', her bulbous bow, designed to increase fuel efficiency as she cleaves her way through the waves, is visible.

R. M. S. Scotland, Dock Gates, Grangemouth.

R.R.R.
E.

Dressed all over, Salvesen Line's Royal Mail Steamer, *Scotland*, sails out of the dock gates at Grangemouth at the start of a voyage across the North Sea to Norway.

Looking up the Forth from Grangemouth, Kincardine Bridge is seen here as the sun sets over the river. It is a view much beloved by many Portonians. When it was opened in 1936, Kincardine Bridge was nicknamed the Silver Link, the name still given to the roadhouse at its southern end on the Stirlingshire shore. At the time it was lowest point on the river that the Forth could be crossed by road and its construction led to the withdrawal of the Higgensneuk ferry which had previously plied the route, near where the old inn that served the waiting passengers still survives.

A snowfall added a definite charm to this picture of the Grange Burn.

This farewell aerial view of Grangemouth looks over the narrow waters of the River Carron from the south west. In the foreground, ships can be seen on the stocks of the Grangemouth Dockyard Co., with the Forth & Clyde Canal and the long straight streets of the Old Town beyond.